# FOR GOD

## — SO —

# LOVED

*Blessing to you both as you proclaim all your the Gospel through your many ministry ventures!*

*Nicole*

Written by Nicole Parks

# TABLE OF CONTENTS

# TABLE OF CONTENTS

# INTRODUCTION

You are about to embark on a journey that starts all the way at the beginning, in the book of Genesis, and continues all the way through Revelation. Perhaps this is the first time you've ever sought to understand the Bible as a whole. Maybe you've read it cover to cover multiple times but are just looking to dive a little deeper. Regardless of where you are in your familiarity and desire to understand God's Word, this study will open your eyes to God's heart and character in new and exciting ways. You are in for a treat, a true feast of the Word of God. Before we dive in, here's what you can expect.

There are seven lessons to this study and each lesson is broken down into three sections. Although there is growth opportunity in solo journeys, this study is richer in the context of community. Whether solo or in a group, you may find that each lesson holds too much for discussion. The study can easily be done as 21 shorter lessons for those wanting to go intentionally slower through it. Read the lessons before group and answer the discussion questions. Then, as a group, go through each section and discuss your responses to both the reading and the questions. Don't limit your discussion to just the questions though. Seek to go a little deeper, regardless of your starting point.

Each section starts with a relevant verse from Isaiah. For clarity, Isaiah was a prophet that lived from 741BC to 681BC. That means his messages came about 700 years BEFORE Jesus walked the earth and about 1400 years AFTER Abraham. It's important to keep that time frame in mind as we journey through the rest of the Bible.

At the end of every session, you'll find suggestions for deeper study. Often these will be full versions of stories that are alluded to or quoted in the study, websites, or other outside resources. These are meant to help you gain more understanding on a deeper level than the study itself provides.

Scriptures quoted are all either NIV or TNIV, unless otherwise noted.

# End Goal

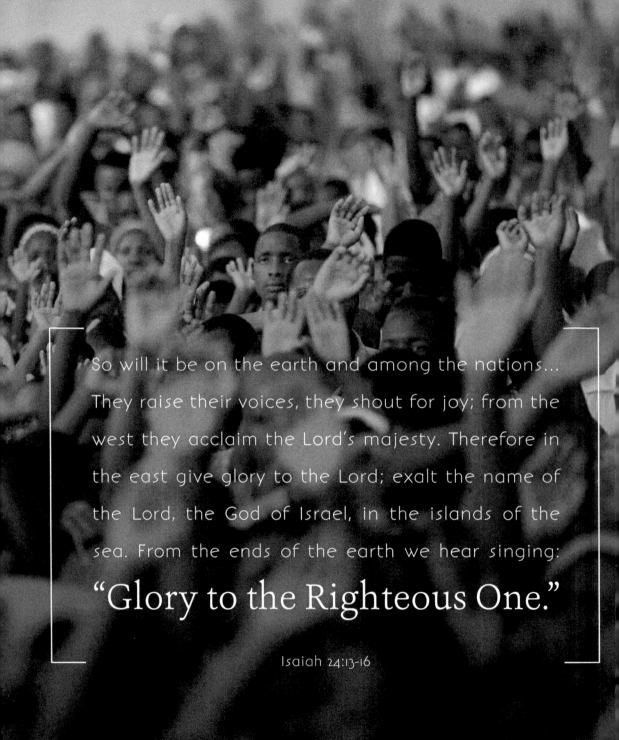

So will it be on the earth and among the nations... They raise their voices, they shout for joy; from the west they acclaim the Lord's majesty. Therefore in the east give glory to the Lord; exalt the name of the Lord, the God of Israel, in the islands of the sea. From the ends of the earth we hear singing: "Glory to the Righteous One."

Isaiah 24:13-16

## - SECTION 1 -
# THE SONG OF THE REDEEMED

Sometimes in life it helps to start with the end in mind. When you know the end goal, or the desired outcome, it is often easier to develop a plan that leads you down the right path. If your goal is "financial freedom", the best way to start toward that goal is to clearly define the end result. For example, one might define financial freedom as being debt-free with a certain amount of money in savings. Defining the goal helps determine the steps that need to be taken in order to achieve it. Another example might be physical health. Setting a vague goal of "being healthier" might not get you very far. However, being intentional about defining the desired end result, like losing 20 pounds or being able to run a marathon by a certain date, gives you a clearer picture of what needs to be done to reach your goal.

What does goal-setting have to do with faith? Most people have probably never considered that the Christian faith has a pre-determined end goal. Thankfully, God has clearly defined His end goal and spelled it out in scripture. Not only that, He also recorded the history of mankind's process and progress towards that goal. In fact, the story of God's work toward this ultimate goal is woven throughout the entire Bible, from Genesis to Revelation. Many Christians go their whole lives without understanding God's purpose and how each and every one of us fits in with that purpose. Once our eyes are opened to the importance of this desired end, every book of the Bible comes together in a way that tells God's story from beginning to end. Are you ready?

The last book of the Bible, Revelation, reads like the script of a weird science fiction movie. It's the final showdown between good and evil, full of unusual imagery and seemingly cryptic messages. Even the author's story sounds like the beginning of a Hollywood blockbuster. John was an outcast and part of a rag tag group of troublemakers called the apostles. He even wrote a book about his time as an apostle, which he creatively titled "John." He fought for his cause his entire life, only to end up exiled on the island of Patmos, where he had a strange vision and encounter with the Lord. The book of Revelation recounts the mysteries that were revealed to him during that divine encounter. One of these great mysteries is God's end goal. In his vision, John is taken into the throne room of heaven where he sees a picture of this completed purpose:

There before me was a great multitude that no one could count, from every nation, tribe, people and language, standing before the throne and in front of the Lamb. They were wearing white robes and were holding palm branches in their hands. And they cried out in a loud voice: "Salvation belongs to our God, who sits on the throne, and to the Lamb."

Rev 7:9

This is God's ultimate goal: redemption. He longs to see people of every nation, tribe, and language represented in heaven, basking in His glory and singing His praise around the throne. This has been God's goal since the fall of man...to redeem His people and bring them back to Him. This was God's purpose in sending His Son to die...to redeem His people so that they "shall not perish but have everlasting life" (John 3:16). Throughout the ages, God has preserved stories and letters and prophecies and scriptures that illustrate how He has been working toward this end goal since the beginning of time.

## DISCUSSION QUESTIONS

**1** Have you ever considered that God might have an end goal, or has the history of mankind seemed arbitrary and pointless?

**2** If we believe that God is all-knowing, He would've been able to see the fall of man. Why did He create man in the first place? Why, knowing the fall would happen, did He still choose to create mankind?

**3** For ages, people have pondered and philosophized over "the meaning of life". Have you ever thought about the meaning of life? If so, what theories have you come up with and what led to those conclusions?

ARISE, SHINE, for your
light has come,
AND THE GLORY OF THE
LORD RISES UPON YOU.
See, darkness covers the earth and
thick darkness is over the peoples,
BUT THE LORD
RISES UPON YOU AND
his glory
appears over you.
Nations will come to your light,
and kings to the
BRIGHTNESS OF
YOUR DAWN.

Isaiah 60:1-3

# - SECTION 2 -
# WORTHY OF PRAISE

If you grew up in church, you may have heard somewhere along the lines that heaven is like a Sunday morning church service for all of eternity. For many people, that picture of heaven doesn't offer much in terms of motivation to spend an eternity there. Will there be hymnals or a hip new-age band? Will it be one of those church services that doubles as your weekly workout? You know the ones, where the leaders tell you to stand up, sit down, kneel, stand up, sit down, stand up, kneel. In heaven's eternal church service, what will the message be like? Loud and convicting? Entertaining and relevant? Long-winded and boring? The imagery from Revelation 7:9 certainly promotes the "heaven is church" theory. Who is this God anyway, who created mankind with the end goal of sitting on His throne and receiving worship from them? Is He some sort of narcissistic being, rewarding those that worship Him and cursing those that don't?

Sometimes we forget the unbelievable worthiness of God. Or perhaps we don't forget as much as we never seek to fully understand. Maybe we understand and simply become accustomed to it, to the point where it becomes commonplace. It's like someone who loves the beach and gets to go once or twice a year. When you arrive and take that first step onto the sand, every aspect of it is captivating. The feel of the sand in your toes, the warm sunshine on your skin, the rhythmic lulling sound of the waves crashing on the shore, the smell of the salty sea air. And of course, the view. Looking out over the vastness of the glistening water until it meets the bright blue sky. It's mesmerizing. Do you know what happens when you move to the beach? It loses its luster just a little bit. You become so accustomed to the sounds that you don't even notice them anymore. Try as you might, you can't even smell that once distinct "beach smell". Even the beauty of the scenery changes, as it simply becomes the background of your everyday life. Perhaps sometimes we unintentionally view God the same way, as merely the background of our everyday life. It is worth the time to intentionally re-focus our senses to the worthiness of God, so let's kick off our shoes, wiggle our toes in the sand, and breathe in the fragrance of the Almighty.

## WHO IS GOD?

GOD IS... omnipotent, meaning He is all-powerful. "For by him all things were created: things in heaven and on earth, visible and invisible, whether thrones or powers or rulers or authorities; all things were created by him and for him" (Colossians 1:16). He alone has "established his throne in heaven, and his kingdom rules over all" (Psalm 103:19)...yet He knows us intimately, having orchestrated every detail of our being. He knit us together in our mothers' wombs (Psalm 139:13), and has even numbered the very hairs on our heads (Matthew 10:29-31).

GOD IS... omniscient, meaning He is all-knowing. "Nothing in all creation is hidden from God's sight" (Hebrews 4:13). In fact, He knows everything about you, when you sit and when you rise, every thought you've ever had (Psalm 139:1-2)...yet He loves you with an everlasting love (Jeremiah 31:3), and He delights in lavishing His love upon us, having us call Him "Abba, Father" which more accurately translates to "Daddy" (1 John 3:1).

GOD IS... omnipresent, meaning He is everywhere at once...yet He chose you the believer as His holy temple, sending His spirit to dwell inside you (1 Corinthians 3:16). God is eternal and unchanging (Psalm 102:12, 27). "The heavens declare the glory of God," (Psalm 19:1), "the whole earth is full of [His] glory," (Isaiah 6:3), and yet He is mindful of human beings, mere mortals, so much so that He crowned us with glory and honor and made us rulers over the works of His hands (Psalm 8:4-6).

GOD IS... holy (Psalm 99), perfect (Psalm 18:30) and good (Psalm 145). He hates sin (Proverbs 8:13) and is justified in holding His creation up to whatever standard He chooses...yet He longs to forgive us of all of our sin and reconcile us to Himself. He chooses not to "treat us as our sins deserve or repay us according to our iniquities" (Psalm 103:10). He tells us that He is not counting our sins against us and has instead made a way for reconciliation (2 Corinthians 5:18-19).

This is a God worthy of praise. This is why, as John recorded in Revelation 4:11, every living creature that surrounded the throne of God cried out "You are worthy, our Lord and God, to receive glory and honor and power, for you created all things, and by your will they were created and have their being."

How great you are, Sovereign Lord! There is no one like you, and there is no God but you, as we have heard with our own ears.

2 Samuel 7:22

The heavens declare the glory of God; the skies proclaim the work of his hands. Day after day they pour forth speech; night after night they display knowledge. They have no speech, they use no words; no sound is heard from them. Yet their voice goes out into all the Earth, their words to the ends of the world.

Psalm 19:1-4

# DISCUSSION QUESTIONS

**1** Do you think that we lose sight of the greatness of God? Why or why not?

**2** Discuss the difference between God being worthy of our praise because of the things He has done versus Him being worthy of praise simply because of who He is, His character. Is one better or more appropriate than the other?

**3** Do you truly believe that God is worthy of our praise?

**4** Does an earthly father have a right to hold his children to a standard of ethics or morality? Does God, as our Creator and our heavenly Father, have a right to hold us to a standard of ethics or morality? Why or why not?

Then all mankind

will know that

I, the LORD,

am your SAVIOR,

your REDEEMER,

the MIGHTY ONE

of Jacob.

Isaiah 49:26

# FOR GOD SO LOVED

The very same John that stood in the throne room of God, watching the completion of God's greatest goal of having worship from every people group, penned the most oft-quoted verse in scripture. "For God so loved the world that He gave His one and only Son, that whoever believes in him shall not perish but have everlasting life" (John 3:16). This verse is another prime example of how repetition can often lead to a mindset of diminished worth. God loves the world. The Greek noun for "world" is found 78 times in the gospel of John and another 24 times in his letters. It can mean the universe, the earth, all of the people on the earth, most of the people, people opposed to God, or the human system opposed to God's purposes.* God's love is not limited to one version of that word. He loves every single person that has ever lived and that ever will live. He loves them uniquely and individually. He loves each and every one, regardless of how they feel about Him. Like a good Father, He loves His children not because of or in spite of anything they have done. He loves His children simply because they are His children. He also loves mankind as a whole. And God loves the nations. His desire, as shown in Revelation 7:9, is to have individuals from each and every nation that make up the whole of mankind become reconciled to Himself.

That intention of reconciliation has been on His heart since before there was even a need for it. The apostle John starts his gospel by saying "In the beginning was the Word, and the Word was with God, and the Word was God. He was with God in the beginning... the Word became flesh and made his dwelling among us. We have seen his glory, the glory of the one and only Son, who came from the Father" (John 1:1-2, 14). Think about that for a minute. The Word, who is Jesus, was with God in the beginning of creation.

*TNIV Study Bible (Zondervan, 2006)

Jesus, the one in whom we find our redemption, whose life's purpose was to show the world the Father's perfect love, was there with God before the foundation of the earth. The apostle Peter confirmed this truth in 1 Peter 1:20, saying "He was chosen before the creation of the world, but was revealed in these last times for your sake." For God so loved the world that He created a redemption plan before sin necessitated redemption.

# DISCUSSION QUESTIONS

**1** Would you characterize the God of the New Testament as a loving God? What about the God of the Old Testament? Why or why not?

**2** How have you experienced the uniquely personal love of God in your life?

**3** How have you seen the corporate or macro love of God, His love for the entire world?

# LESSON 1
# FOR DEEPER STUDY

● Read Revelation chapter 5.
Who is the Root of David?

Compare what you read in Revelation 5 with what Jesus says about authority in Matthew 28:18.

● In Revelation 5:9 it says "with your blood you purchased for God members of every tribe and language and people and nation." In your own words, what does this mean?

● Read Daniel 7:9-14.
Who is the Son of Man? Compare verse 14 with Revelation 5.

Compare this dream given to the prophet Daniel hundreds of years before Jesus walked the earth to the vision John had in Revelation 5, specifically verse 9.

- Read Matthew 26:62-64. As Jesus is being tried by the Sanhedrin, how does his response correspond with the prophecies in Revelation 5:9 and Daniel 7:9-14?

- Read Revelation 4:6-11. Why might the four creatures look upon the Lord day and night and never be able to stop praising Him?

In verse 11, why do the elders say God is worthy of praise?

LESSON 2

# THE PROMISE OF BLESSING

If only you had paid attention to my commands,

your peace would have
been like a river,

your well-being like the waves of the sea.

Isaiah 48:18

# - SECTION 1 -
# IN THE BEGINNING

We've probably all read the first few chapters of Genesis. Maybe, if you're just being honest, you've read them more than any other chapters in the Bible. Not necessarily because of the riveting nature of the story but because maybe you've resolved more New Years Days than you care to remember to read the Bible cover to cover. You start out great those first few days or weeks in January but pretty soon you bump into the less-than riveting tales of exact measurements for a temple or 600+ laws or perhaps the book of the census list that reads like a phone book. Whatever the case may be, the Bible is an intimidating book. Technically, it's an intimidating collection of books, letters, and historical documents, 66 to be exact. The good news is that it doesn't have to be so intimidating. Once the big picture story of God is understood, it's easier to appreciate, understand, and at times push through the individual books of the Bible.

The entire Bible tells the story of God redeeming His people. We all know the story of Adam and Eve's fall from grace all too well. God created them to be in fellowship and intimate relationship with Him. In Genesis 3:8 we see God's desire for intimacy with His creation. It says, "Then the man and his wife heard the sound of the Lord God as he was walking in the garden in the cool of the day." God could've been off somewhere on His throne, enjoying the worship of the angels or out creating new galaxies or new species of animals but instead He was casually walking in the garden, looking for His companions. God never intended to be a God of rules. He only had one in the beginning and like all future rules, it was not intended to keep something good from them but to protect them from something He knew would harm them. Like a father teaching his children not to run into the street, the intent is not to keep something good and fun from them

Genesis 3:21 is an often overlooked glimpse into the character of God. It says "The Lord God made garments of skin for Adam and his wife and clothed them." Before they ate the forbidden fruit, they knew no shame. They didn't know they were "supposed" to be ashamed of being naked. The moment they took a bite, the moment sin entered the world, sin's constant companion, shame, entered with it. Yet still God, in His infinite mercy and love, chose to cover the shame of their nakedness. One day He would once and for all cover the sin and shame of the entire world with His abundant mercy and unending love.

but rather to protect them from danger they are unable to see. The forbidden fruit basically opened their eyes to the difference between good and evil. God knew that this would lead to His creation thinking they didn't need Him, like a defiant toddler insistent on crossing the street alone. Our Father knew this world is navigated best by trusting in Him, allowing Him to gently and lovingly lead us. Unfortunately, God's children chose to believe that He did not have their best interests at heart. They believed the lie that He could not be trusted, that He was keeping something good from them. Isn't it ironic that the same lie still runs rampant today? Despite the fact that Adam and Eve disobeyed God, in His infinite grace and mercy He still determined to redeem His people back into relationship with Himself.

In the midst of God's curse on the serpent, we see a foreshadowing of His great redemption plan. In Genesis 3:15, God says to the serpent "I will put enmity between you and the woman, and between your offspring and hers; he will crush your head, and you will strike his heel." God was telling the enemy "you will wound my son...but my Son will destroy you". And we know that that is exactly what happened on a sinner's cross at Calvary thousands of years later.

# DISCUSSION QUESTIONS

**1** Jesus, who was without sin but became sin for our redemption, was with God before sin existed. What is the significance of knowing that the solution to the sin problem existed before the problem itself?

**2** Read Genesis 3:21. What does it say to you personally about the character of God that He chose to clothe them, to cover up their shame, before sending them away?

**3** Do you feel that God is able and willing to cover up your shame?

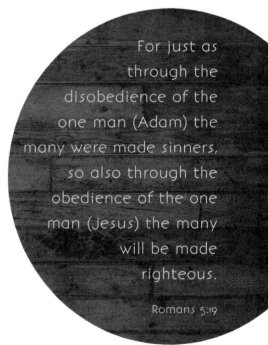

For just as through the disobedience of the one man (Adam) the many were made sinners, so also through the obedience of the one man (Jesus) the many will be made righteous.

Romans 5:19

IN MY FAITHFULNESS

I will reward
my people and
MAKE AN EVERLASTING
COVENANT WITH THEM.
Their descendants will be known
among the nations and their
offspring among the peoples.
ALL WHO SEE THEM WILL
ACKNOWLEDGE THAT THEY ARE A
people the Lord has
BLESSED.

Isaiah 61:8-9

## — SECTION 2 —
# BLESSED TO BE
# A BLESSING

The beginning of God's great redemption plan in action was a promise. It was a promise to Abraham, with a purpose, and a foreshadowing of God's salvation through grace. In Genesis 12:2-3, God's plan began to take shape.

> I will make you into a great nation,
> and I will bless you;
> I will make your name great,
> And you will be a blessing.
> I will bless those who bless you,
> And whoever curses you I will curse;
> And all peoples on earth
> Will be blessed through you.

This promise to Abraham became the turning point of all human history. Before God made this promise to Abraham (who was at that point called Abram), the Bible tells us very little about the man who would become the father of this great nation. Essentially, God showed up and said to Abraham "Follow me", a call His Son would make to a few unimpressive, unknown, regular guys thousands of years later. But Abraham's command to follow came with a promise. God told Abraham that He would bless him so *that* all people on earth would be blessed.

# ACTIVITY

Look back on the above verse. Underline the statements that are promises exclusively given to Abraham. Double underline the statements that show outcomes beyond Abraham's life.

The statement of promise ("I will make you into a great nation, and I will bless you") came with a clearly connected purpose ("you will be a blessing" and "all peoples on earth will be blessed through you"). God was putting into action His plan of redeeming His people back to Him and He was starting with Abraham.

# DISCUSSION QUESTIONS

**1** Abraham was neither blessed because of something he did nor because of any favor he had earned with the Lord. He was blessed in order to be a blessing to others. Discuss this idea of "being blessed in order to be a blessing."

**2** Do you think that this same concept applies to us today? Why or why not?

Turn to me and be saved,

all you ends of the earth; for I am God, and there
is no other. By myself I have sworn, my mouth has
uttered in all integrity a word that will not be
revoked: Before me every knee will bow; by me
every tongue will swear.

Isaiah 45:22-23

# - SECTION 3 -
# CREDITED AS RIGHTEOUSNESS

Righteousness. It's a word tossed around in church circles, some more than others, and it is seen throughout the Bible as something to be strived for...but do we really understand what righteousness is? The dictionary defines it as being upright, moral, virtuous, or justifiable. The TNIV Study Bible defines it as the state of being perfect and without sin. What it really boils down to in terms of its prevalent use in the Scriptures is having a right standing with God. When things are well and right between you and the holy God, you have a righteousness with Him. After God gave His initial promise of blessing to Abraham in Genesis chapter 12, God promised him that his offspring would be more numerous than the stars in the sky (15:5). Then "Abram believed the Lord, and He credited it to him as righteousness" (15:6). This was the first time that scripture shows God responding to faith by crediting the believer with righteousness. God made a promise to Abraham, Abraham believed God, God credited Abraham with a right-standing and redeemed relationship simply based on his faith. God's interaction and relationship with Abraham was foreshadowing the relationship Jesus would have with His followers. This comes full circle to Jesus in Romans 4:23-24, "The words 'it was credited to him' were written not for him alone, but also for us, to whom God will credit righteousness-for us who believe in him who raised Jesus our Lord from the dead." God began something through Abraham that He completed through Jesus...a righteousness, a right-standing with God, available to ALL people on earth who believe. God told Abraham to leave everything to follow Him, just as Jesus did to His disciples. Abraham, through faith, became the father of all who believe in God. God blessed Abraham so that through him the rest of the earth could experience a redeemed relationship with a loving heavenly Father.

Four more times in Genesis, God repeated this solemn oath to Abraham and his sons (Genesis 18:18, 22:16-18, 26:3-5, 28:13-14). Anything of great importance bears repeating. The third time He said it, He even added a little extra emphasis to it by saying "I swear by myself..." (22:16). That might sound odd, that He would swear to it by Himself...but after all, He is God. There is no name higher than His own with which He can take an oath.

## DISCUSSION QUESTIONS

**1** Do you think that you have a righteousness, or right-standing, with the Lord? Why or why not?

**2** What can we do to earn or merit having a righteousness with a holy and blameless God?

LESSON 2
# FOR DEEPER STUDY

● Read the following verses and write the command that God gave in each.

– Genesis 1:28

– Genesis 9:1

– Genesis 9:6-7

● Read the story of the Tower of Babel in Genesis 11:1-9. As we read in the previous verses, God's plan was to have mankind "multiply and subdue the earth." He wanted to fill the earth with His image-bearers. In Genesis 11:4, how did the building of the Tower of Babel stand in direct opposition to God's command?

● Read Genesis 12:1. What is God asking Abram to do in this verse? What is Abram's response in verse 4?

- Re-read Genesis 12:2-3, also known as the Abrahamic Covenant. What are the three ways that God says He would bless Abraham? What is His purpose in blessing him and his descendants?

- What does God promise Abraham in Genesis 18:18?

- Read Genesis 22. How does the story of Abraham's obedience with his son foreshadow Jesus?

- Specifically in Genesis 22:5, read what Abraham said to his servants. How does what he said to his servants underscore the definition of faith in Hebrews 11:1?

● Read Galatians 3:7-14 where Paul explains the Abrahamic Covenant. How does this help define, redefine, or clarify the gospel of Jesus? How does this explanation affect the relevancy of the Old Testament in light of the Gospel?

LESSON 3

# SET APART

Does the clay say to the potter, 'What are you making?' Does your work say, 'The potter has no hands'? This is what the Lord says—the Holy One of Israel, and its Maker: Concerning things to come, do you question me about my children, or give me orders about

the work of my hands?

Isaiah 45:9-11

# THE NATION OF ISRAEL

Shakespeare once said, "That which we call a rose, by any other name would smell as sweet." Although a name does not define us, we know that names can have very significant meanings. This was especially true in Biblical times. Names were given based on family lineage, the feelings of someone's parents or circumstances at birth, a historical situation at the time of birth, or even a prophetic meaning around how a person's life would unfold. Often times, as we saw with Abraham, God would give people new names to signify new roles in their lives. Abram, meaning "exalted father" became Abraham, meaning "father of many", when God gave him the promise of blessing (Genesis 17). Abraham did in fact become the father of many. To this day, he is credited as the father of Christianity, Judaism, and Islam. Maybe you've heard God referred to as "the God of Abraham, Isaac, and Jacob". Isaac was born to Abraham and Sarah (once called Sarai) when they were well advanced in age (Genesis 21). (In case you were wondering, "well advanced in age" is the politically correct way of saying they were old. Very old.) Isaac married a woman named Rebekah (Genesis 24) and she had twin boys, Jacob and Esau. Through some not-so-friendly sibling rivalry, Jacob (the younger twin) stole his older brother's birthright and blessing. But we know that "in all things God works for the good of those who love him, who have been called according to his purpose" (Romans 8:28).

In Genesis chapter 28, Jacob left home, fleeing from the wrath of his brother. (Apparently even then little brothers knew there was only so far you could push your big brother before he came after you.) One night during his travels, Jacob had a dream. In it, God said to him:

I am the Lord, the God of your father Abraham and the God of Isaac. I will give you and your descendants the land on which you are lying. Your descendants will be like the dust of the earth, and you will spread out to the west and to the east, to the north and to the south. All peoples on earth will be blessed through you and your offspring. I am with you, and will watch over you wherever you go, and I will bring you back to this land. I will not leave you until I have done what I have promised you.

Genesis 28:13-15

All 3 of these fathers of our faith, Abraham, Isaac, and Jacob (also known as the patriarchs), married women who the Bible refers to as barren or childless at some point. Yet they all conceived and gave birth in God's timing, according to His plan. The answer to each of their unfulfilled longings was an integral part of God's bigger purposes. Have you ever considered how God might use your unfulfilled longings for His bigger purpose?

Sound familiar? This is the same blessing God gave to Abraham, the promise of blessing with a purpose. Jacob would be blessed in order to be a blessing. Many years and 12 sons later, God changed Jacob's name to Israel. His 12 sons would become the 12 tribes of Israel, also known as the Israelites. Thus God had made a name for His people and a people for His name.

# DISCUSSION QUESTIONS

**1** Does your name or the name(s) you picked out for your children have any special meaning?

**2** Often our titles and/or relationships can become the name by which we are more commonly known. For example, so-and-so's mom/sister/daughter/wife, so-and-so's husband/son/father, Dr. Smith, Mr. Jones, etc. What names have you gone by that you feel proud to bear? What names have you had to bear unwillingly or with shame?

**3** Why do you think God puts such an emphasis on a person's name?

God continued to bless the Israelites as He had promised to the patriarchs and after a few generations, they had indeed become a great nation in a strange land. The Israelites became such a great nation after relocating to Egypt that they began to outnumber the Egyptians themselves. As history has shown time and time again, the Egyptians became less tolerant of the "them" threatening their cultural identity. The book of Exodus opens with the nation of Israel, once a blessed people in a foreign land, now a nation of slaves living under Egyptian oppression. The new pharaoh became so threatened by the growing nation of Israel that he instated an order that called for the murder of all male babies born to an Israelite. Through the will of God, a baby named Moses would not only survive the infant genocide, but would be raised in the palace by Pharaoh's daughter (Exodus 1-2).

Years later, through a mighty display of God's power and might, Moses led the Israelites out from under the heavy yoke of Egyptian slavery, across a dried up Red Sea, and on a quest for the land God had promised their forefathers (Exodus 4-13). After the dust settled a bit from their mighty exodus, God revealed His purpose in choosing the nation of Israel as His own people:

> This is what you (Moses) are to say to the house of Jacob and what you are to tell the people of Israel: "You yourselves have seen what I (the Lord) did to Egypt, and how I carried you on eagles' wings and brought you to myself. Now if you obey me fully and keep my covenant, then out of all nations you will be my treasured possession. Although the whole earth is mine, you will be for me a kingdom of priests and a holy nation.
>
> Exodus 19:3-6

We know that the Israelites were God's chosen people but why? For what purpose were they chosen? God does not do anything arbitrarily. As we saw in God's promise to Abraham, God blessed in two ways: in response to faith and with a purpose. God blessed Abraham because of his faith, not because of his works or his actions. He did it with the intention of that blessing being used to bless others. We see the same thing happening here with the Israelites. God blessed them by rescuing them from slavery and bringing them to Himself before they "earned" anything. Then in Exodus 19:3-6 we see the purpose…to be for God "a kingdom of priests and a holy nation". They were set apart to be priests, wholly consecrated to God's service, and vessels of God's grace to the rest of the world. We see this purpose reiterated in 1 Peter 2:9, "But you are a chosen people, a royal priesthood, a holy nation, God's special possession, [so] that you might declare the praises of Him who called you out of darkness into His wonderful light." God set apart the Israelites then and the followers of Jesus now for one purpose…to show the world the great love of the one true God.

# DISCUSSION QUESTIONS

**1** When you hear the word priest or pastor, what responsibilities do you think of in regards to those roles?

**2** What do you think it would it look like for an entire group of people, a nation of people, to take on the role of priest or pastor?

**3** How would your community or nation look differently if you lived as a community or nation of priests?

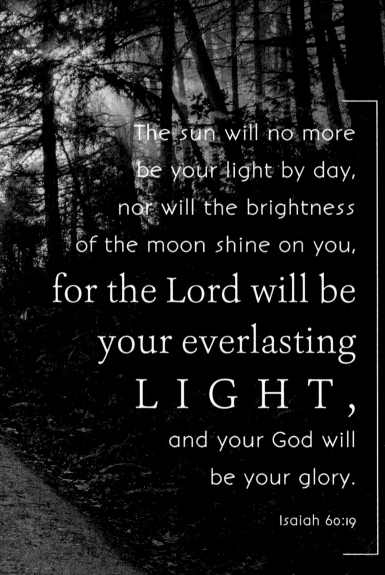

The sun will no more
be your light by day,
nor will the brightness
of the moon shine on you,
for the Lord will be
your everlasting
L I G H T,
and your God will
be your glory.

Isaiah 60:19

## - SECTION 3 -
# THE JOURNEY BEGINS

Have you ever played the game where you are blindfolded and paired up with a partner who is responsible for being your eyes? Basically the partner without the blindfold is responsible for directing the temporarily blinded partner to whatever is the end goal. It requires a tremendous amount of trust on behalf of the blindfolded party and a tremendous amount of foresight and care on behalf of the party with unimpaired vision. After the Israelites left Egypt, God played the role of the partner with sight as His people learned how to trust Him and follow Him without seeing the process, the hindrances, or the finish line. In Exodus chapter 16 we are introduced to manna. Manna was the bread of heaven that the Bible says "tasted like wafers made with honey" (Exodus 16:31). Every morning, God would provide only as much manna as they needed for the day. God was teaching them how trust Him for their daily bread (Sound familiar? In what most people know as The Lord's Prayer, Jesus taught His followers to pray for their daily bread in Matthew 6:9-13). God went before them as their guide, in the form of a pillar of cloud by day and a pillar of fire by night (Exodus 13:21-22). Never once did God leave them. God gave them instructions on how to build a holy tent, called a tabernacle, for His presence to reside in. It was God's desire to make His dwelling among them (Exodus 25:8). God also began the process of purifying His chosen people through an extensive list of laws.

The word tabernacle means a dwelling place, though it is rarely used in reference to human dwellings in the Bible. Throughout scripture it almost always signifies the place where God dwells among His people. Four times in the Old Testament and twice in the New Testament, we see evidence of God's desire to "tabernacle" among His people.

As we read in Exodus 19:3-6, God was creating a "holy nation" in order to have them serve as His "kingdom of priests". God did not give the nation of Israel 600+ laws as a way for them to earn His love and favor. He had already proven His love and favor by remembering His people, rescuing them from slavery, delivering them from oppression, providing for them financially (Exodus 12:35-36), providing for their physical needs (Exodus 16-17), and making His Holy dwelling among them.

I, the Lord, have called you in righteousness;
    I will take hold of your hand.
I will keep you and will make you
        to be a covenant for the people
        and a light for the Gentiles,
to open eyes that are blind,
        to free captives from prison
        and to release from the dungeon
those who sit in darkness.

Isaiah 42:6-7

# DISCUSSION QUESTIONS

**1** Talk about the relationship and rules that existed in your family of origin. Were the rules in your home excessive, non-existent, or somewhere in between? Were they enforced authoritatively, lackadaisically, or lovingly? How has that affected your view of God's "rules"?

**2** Give an example of a rule that you have lived or worked under that seemed entirely unnecessary or excessive at one time but that you grew to appreciate later.

# FOR DEEPER STUDY

● Read Genesis 32:22-30. What is the meaning of the name Israel?

● As we've seen, God set apart the nation of Israel for His purposes. In light of that purpose, what do you think is the significance of God changing Jacob's name to Israel?

● Read Genesis 35:9-12. What is the command given to Jacob/Israel in these verses?

● Read the story of Joseph in Genesis chapters 35 through 45. Reflect on all the oppression and false accusation that Joseph endured. How did he respond to it all? (Genesis 39:2-9, 20-23;41:39-40, 51-52)

● What did Joseph say was the ultimate purpose in everything he endured? (Genesis 45:4-7)

● God continued to bless the nation of Israel in order to draw the nations to Himself. Observe how this played out in the following stories:

– The plagues of Egypt (Exodus 5:1-2; 7:5, 17; 8:10, 19; 9:13-17, 29)

– The exodus from Egypt (Exodus 12:38; 14:4, 17-18)

– The parting of the Red Sea (Exodus 14:31; Joshua 4:23-24, 2:8-11)

– Moses and his father-in-law Jethro (Exodus 18:7-12)

– The rules and commands God gave the nation of Israel (Deuteronomy 4:5-8)

# PROMISES,
# PROVISION,
# AND
# PREPARATION

HE WILL TEACH US HIS WAYS,

SO THAT WE MAY WALK IN

HIS PATHS.

THE LAW WILL GO OUT FROM ZION,

THE WORD OF THE LORD FROM

JERUSALEM.

Isaiah 2:3

# WANDERING IN THE DESERT

The Israelites wandered through the desert on their way to the Promised Land for 40 years. When you look at the route they took, it's clear that the journey took place well before GPS. Deuteronomy 1:2 alludes to the fact that it should've taken days from Mount Sinai, not years. Why would God lead them on the most inefficient route possible? Surely there must've been a more direct route from Egypt to Jericho? The book of Deuteronomy, the 5th book of the Bible, opens up with Moses giving a powerful pep talk to the Israelites. In fact, most of the book of Deuteronomy consists of speeches Moses delivered to the generation of Israelites that would soon cross into the Promised Land. They were on the brink of crossing into the land flowing with milk and honey and their fearless leader stopped them for a brief history lesson to realign their vision with God's purpose. Moses wanted to make sure that they were ready for what was ahead. In this speech, he reminded the people of their rebellion and distrust in the Lord. You see, God's original intention was not to have them wander in the desert for 40 years. Unfortunately, the Israelites did not prove themselves trustworthy. As Jesus would reiterate much later through a parable in Luke chapter 12, God expects much accountability from those who are entrusted with much. God was planning on blessing the Israelites abundantly with land and wealth and influence and long lives marked by good health. All of this was promised in exchange for obedience in order to show the other nations the nearness and provision of their God, the God who loves His people.

*Observe [the decrees and laws] carefully, for this will show your wisdom and understanding to the nations, who will hear about all these decrees and say "Surely this great nation is a wise and understanding people." What other nation is so great as to have their gods near them the way the Lord our God is near us whenever we pray to Him?*

Deuteronomy 4:6-7

God was going to use the nation of Israel as a beacon of light for the other nations. He wanted them, as He said through the prophet Daniel, to "shine as bright as the sky, and [to] lead many to righteousness, [and] shine like the stars forever" (Daniel 12:3). God was calling them to a mission that was uniquely and divinely His. They would be blessed in order to be a blessing. He was going to use them to bring the nations of the world back to Himself. In order to do that, they had to trust Him implicitly, follow Him blindly, and obey Him humbly. Despite the fact that they had seen many wonders performed by His hand, they had seen and heard His daily presence (Deuteronomy 4:14), He had rescued them from slavery, He had blessed the work of their hands, watched over their journey (Deuteronomy 2:7), He had delivered them through war, and He had provided food and water on their journey, they still lacked the blind faith and obedience He deserved. God proved Himself worthy of praise so that Israel would know and understand His authority. He told them in Deuteronomy 4:32-40, that there is a direct correlation between obeying His commands and living well in the Promised Land. Yet the people were rebellious and they lacked trust in God. So for 40 years, God led them blindly through the desert, teaching the next generation the importance of all these things, of trust and obedience. Then, just before crossing into the land of blessing, He had His servant Moses reiterate everything He had shown them and taught them in those 40 years. It was as if He wanted to look each person in the eyes and say, "This is important! Listen to me! I'm doing something through you that has been planned since the beginning of time. I am redeeming my people, bringing them back to me, and showing them that there is no God besides me, the God who loves them."

# DISCUSSION QUESTIONS

**1** Looking back throughout your life, have you walked through any seasons of wandering and waiting? What are some of the lessons God taught you during that season? How was it used for His glory? How might you have reacted to it differently if you knew then what you know now?

Has any other god ever tried to take for himself one nation out of another nation, by testings, by signs and wonders, by war, by a mighty hand and an outstretched arm, or by great and awesome deeds, like all the things the Lord your God did for you in Egypt before your very eyes? You were shown these things so that you might know that the Lord is God: besides him there is no other.

Deuteronomy 4:33-35

land flowing with milk and honey." For a nation that had been under the heavy yoke of slavery in a foreign land for generations, it was a land to call their own. Yet the purpose of the blessing never changed...they were blessed to be a blessing. God was raising up a nation of priests, placing them at the center of the known world, displaying through them His splendor and power and glory, in order to make them a light for the nations so that His "salvation [might] reach to the ends of the earth" (Isaiah 49:6).

# ACTIVITY

Read Psalm 67 and underline the two statements of purpose. (Hint: they both begin with "so that".) Now double underline the actions that bring about those statements of purpose.

May God be gracious to us and bless us
    and make his face shine upon us—
so that your ways may be known on earth,
    your salvation among all nations.
May the peoples praise you, God;
    may all the peoples praise you.
May the nations be glad and sing for joy,
    for you rule the peoples with equity
    and guide the nations of the earth.
May the peoples praise you, God;
    may all the people praise you.
The land yields its harvest;
    God, our God, blesses us.
May God bless us still,
    so that all the ends of the earth will fear him.

Psalm 67

In both statements of purpose, we see once again how God is working towards accomplishing His purpose...He is blessing His people so that they will bless others and bring glory to Him. He blesses His people so that His name would be known among all people throughout the world. God did not choose to bless Abraham for the benefit of Abraham. He did not choose to bless the Israelites solely for the benefit of the Israelites. In Deuteronomy 9:6, He says to the Israelites "Understand, then, that it is not because of your righteousness that the Lord your God is giving you this good land to possess, for you are a stiff-necked people." God's purpose in blessing is always for the benefit of all peoples on earth, otherwise known as the nations. God wanted his favor to his people to be so obviously from Him that all the other nations on earth would take notice and turn in His direction.

What about the nations that the Israelites drove out and destroyed? Through their conquest of the Promised Land, God commanded the Israelites to destroy and kill many nations of people. If God loved "the nations" so much, why was the Promised Land taken through violent means? There's often a tension, or a misconception, between seeing the loving Father portrayed in the New Testament and the angry, vengeful God of the Old Testament. In Deuteronomy 9:4, God reiterated that its not because of any righteousness of the Israelites that they were able to take the Promised Land from its former inhabitants but rather it was "on account of the wickedness of these nations that the Lord [drove] them out." Archeologists have discovered ancient ruins and original literature from these people that suggest that these early nations worshipped many false gods through practices that included religious prostitution and child sacrifice. Instead of allowing them to remain in the prime location for their wickedness to spread throughout the world, God gave the land to His nation of priests.

# SEA TRADE ROUTES OF THE PHOENICIANS

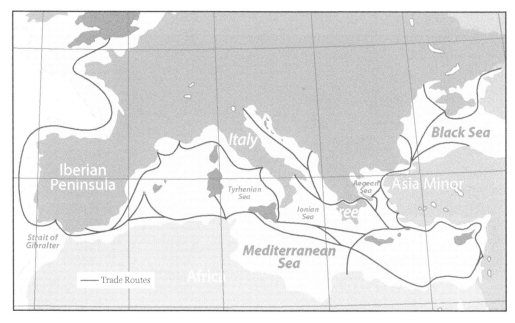

This map shows the sea trade of the Phoenicians, who are credited with the development of what became commerce and the written alphabet. They were also the traders that supplied the "cedars of Lebanon" used in building the tabernacle and later the temple. Their reach went throughout Europe, northern Africa, the Middle East, and Asia.

# TRADE ROUTES AND GREAT EMPIRES
# OF THE FIRST CENTURY A.D.

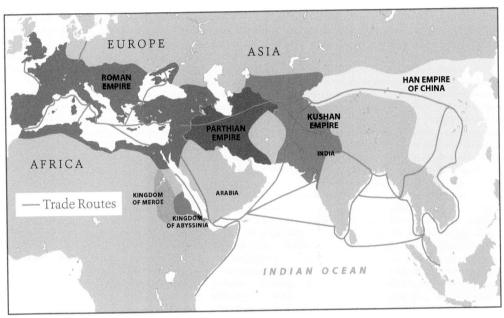

This last map shows the greater picture of trade throughout the known world in the first century. Consider the impact it could've had on the world if the truth of God's great love and desire for redemption had spread along those same routes.

"Do not
be afraid,
you worm Jacob,
little Israel,
do not fear,
for I myself
will help you,"
declares the Lord,
your Redeemer,
the Holy One of Israel.

# FOR US OR AGAINST US?

Every language is filled with colloquialisms and clichés of unknown origin. People might be surprised to know how many English words and phrases actually come from the Bible. Military and political leaders have used the saying "You're either for us or against us" for centuries across the globe. It has been quoted in books, movies, and even cartoons. However, the Bible lays claim on this one. In fact, the Gospels record Jesus saying this four times. (Matthew 12:30; Luke 9:50, 11:23; Mark 9:40) Yet, the first time this phrase appears is way back in the Old Testament from the mouth of Joshua, Moses' successor as the leader of God's people. When the Israelites began their conquest of the Promised Land, God was clear about which nations would be spared and which would not. For many of the existing nations living in the land God would give the Israelites, their sin had reached "its full measure" (Genesis 15:16) and God knew His people

> Jesus is the Greek form of the name Joshua, which means "the Lord saves."

would become easily entangled in that sin if left alone. After they crossed the Jordan River (in the same style they crossed the Red Sea to begin this journey 40 years prior), Joshua found himself face-to-face with a sword-wielding man. Joshua went right up to him and said "Are you for us or for our enemies?" (Joshua 5:13) Joshua was drawing a line in the sand. You're either with us or against us, for us or for our enemies. Throughout the book of Joshua, God's redemption story shines brightly, even amidst the war and violence of conquering the Promised Land. Joshua led God's people into the land of promise, and through that act began reconciling the nations back to God. He was one of the first "good guys", leading his army against evil for the sake of their just and righteous cause.

> [The Lord] gave you a land on which you did not toil and cities you did not build; and you live in them and eat from vineyards and olive groves that you did not plant. Now fear the Lord and serve Him with all faithfulness. Throw away the gods your ancestors worshiped beyond the Euphrates River and in Egypt, and serve the Lord. But if serving the Lord seems undesirable to you, then choose for yourselves this day whom you will serve, whether the gods your ancestors served beyond the Euphrates, or the gods of the Amorites, in whose land you are living. But as for me and my household, we will serve the Lord.
>
> Joshua 24:13-15

The sword-wielding man turned out to be a commander for the army of the Lord. He came to Joshua with instructions on the first conquest and a very unusual plan of attack: Jericho. It was a fortified city just across the Jordan River, booming, bustling, and supplied with water by many strong springs. Joshua had sent two spies in to size up the opposition before them. The spies were well-informed and protected from capture by a prostitute named Rahab. She gave them the information they needed to move forward and in exchange for that, they spared her life and the lives of her family members. The walls of Jericho crumbled at the feet of the Israelite soldiers. Rahab boldly proclaimed her faith in the one true God, the God of Israel, and by faith she was saved. Not only saved but Rahab the Gentile prostitute became one of only five women highlighted in the genealogy of Jesus Christ (Matthew 1:1-16). Her faith in declaring that she was for God wrote her name into the greatest redemption story ever told.

SO LOVED

"Are you for us or for our enemies?"
–Joshua

# DISCUSSION QUESTIONS

1. Read Joshua 5:13-15. Clearly the commander of the Lord's army came to help Joshua and Israelites but where was his primary allegiance? Discuss the significance of how he responded to Joshua.

2. Rahab was the first of many redemption stories that came after the Israelites conquered and inhabited the Promised Land. She was a woman, a Gentile, and a prostitute. Why would God intentionally keep her name in the story and lineage of Jesus? How does the story of Rahab highlight God's love for the nations?

# FOR DEEPER STUDY

- God continued to bless the nation of Israel in order to draw the nations to Himself. Observe how this played out in the following stories:

  - Rahab and the spies (Joshua 2, 6:22-25)

  - Ruth and Naomi (Book of Ruth, specifically 1:16)

  - David and Goliath (1 Samuel 17:46-47)

  - God blessing Solomon (1 Kings 4:29-34; 10:1-9)

  - Queen Esther (Esther 8:15-18)

  - Shadrach, Meshach, and Abednego (Daniel 3, 4:1-3)

  - Daniel and the lion's den (Daniel 6:16-28)

- Read Deuteronomy 1:32-34. What was God trying to teach the Israelites during their journey to the Promised Land?

- Read Deuteronomy 4:32-35 and Ezekiel 20:5-7. Why did God do all of the things listed in this verse? What was His ultimate purpose?

- What was God's offer to Israel in Ezekiel 20:6?

- What was the people's response to God's offer in Ezekiel 20:8?

- Considering his purpose, why was it so detestable to Him for his people Israel to worship false gods and idols?

- Despite the fact that God's people were continually rebellious and repeatedly turned to false gods and idols, why does it say in Ezekiel 20:9 that He rescued and redeemed them?

# STANDING FIRM

HEAR ME, YOU heavens! LISTEN, EARTH! For the Lord has spoken: "I REARED CHILDREN AND BROUGHT THEM UP, but they have rebelled against me. The ox knows its master, the donkey its owner's manger, BUT ISRAEL DOES NOT KNOW, MY PEOPLE DO NOT understand.

Isaiah 1:2-3

# - SECTION 1 -
# REBELLION AND REPENTANCE

History has a way of repeating itself. Basic human nature remains the same because we live in a broken world diseased with sin. God gave us free will because He desires authentic relationship with us, His creation. After all, what value is there in love, trust, and obedience if it is not given voluntarily? He gave us free will so that we could choose to love Him, even knowing that that meant many would choose not to. Unfortunately for the Israelites, after Joshua led the troops in, the very next generation began a vicious cycle that would be repeated throughout the rest of the Old Testament. God's chosen people, His light to the nations, His city on a hill, veered off the course God had for them. They committed to following Him and for a time, enjoyed His blessings and provision. Eventually they became disenchanted with His rules and started believing the lie that He was holding back something good from them. Ultimately they gave in to the temptation to conform to the pagan nations around them and chose a life of sinful godlessness. Sin always has its own consequences and their rebellion would always pull them away from God's blessing and provision. Then they would plead for God's mercy and interventions from deep within the pit of their own sin. For generations, this pattern continued. Rebellion, repentance, redemption, repeat. God foresaw all of it and warned His people through Moses before they even stepped foot into the Promised Land (Deuteronomy 4:25-31). Despite all of their rebellion, God continued to love them and show mercy on His chosen people. Although God required obedience from His people, it was never a

> But the plans of the Lord stand firm forever, the purposes of his heart through all generations.
>
> Psalm 33:11

The Old Testament is broken up into five sections. Although some of the books are in chronological order, the majority of the Old Testament is not organized that way. The first five books are called the Pentateuch, which is the law. (Genesis-Deuteronomy) Then there are 12 books of history. (Joshua-Esther) Next are five poetic and wisdom books. (Job-Song of Solomon) Lastly, the 17 books of the major and minor prophets. (Isaiah-Malachi)

prerequisite for His love. In Deuteronomy 6:24-25, God promised that obedience would lead to a good life and their faith in believing that promise was credited to them as righteousness. However, with each generation that passed, they found themselves further and further from God, further polluted by the world around them.

In the early years in the Promised Land, God raised up judges from among the people to help them interpret and follow God's laws.

Yet they would not listen to their judges but prostituted themselves to other gods and worshiped them. Unlike their ancestors, they quickly turned from following the way of their ancestors, the way of obedience to the Lord's commands...they refused to give up their evil practices and stubborn ways. Therefore the Lord was very angry with Israel and said, "Because this nation has violated the covenant I ordained for their ancestors and has not listened to me, I will no longer drive out before them any of the nations Joshua left when he died. I will use them to test Israel and see whether they will keep the way of the Lord and walk in it as their ancestors did."

Judges 2:16

Notice that He never revoked the covenant or went back on His word. God had sworn an oath by His own name and "He remembered his holy promise given to his servant Abraham" (Psalm 105:42). After the time of the judges, the Israelites wanted a king, so that they would "be like all the other nations" (1 Samuel 8:19-20). Despite warnings from the Lord through His prophet Samuel, they rejected God as their king, they forsook Him, and they served other gods (1 Samuel 8:6-9). Do you see that same lie creeping back in, the first lie that began the separation between God and His creation? The people thought that they did not need God. They believed that He was more interested in keeping something from them than in doing something through them.

> Let all the earth fear the Lord; let all the people of the world revere him.
>
> Psalm 33:8

# DISCUSSION QUESTIONS

1. Read Deuteronomy 4:25-31. What does it say about God's character that He predicted the rebellion of His people and yet foretold how He would be merciful to them?

2. Have you ever made a poor decision but were shown mercy instead of the punishment you deserved? How did that affect your relationship with the person that showed mercy?

**3** Is there anything in your life that you feel has the potential to or already has pulled you outside of God's blessing and provision? What would it look like to be fully repentant of that?

**4** Do you ever see this age-old lie creeping into your life, the lie that we don't need God and that He can't be trusted? Do you find it easy to believe the lie and if so, why do you think that is?

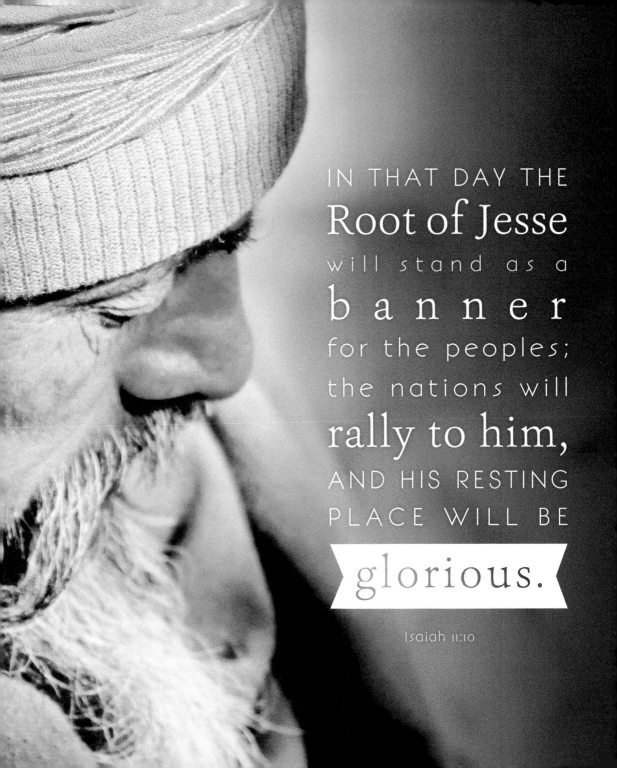

IN THAT DAY THE
Root of Jesse
will stand as a
banner
for the peoples;
the nations will
rally to him,
AND HIS RESTING
PLACE WILL BE
glorious.

Isaiah 11:10

## - SECTION 2 -
# A MAN AFTER GOD'S OWN HEART

As God's chosen people continued to choose their own way, things got progressively worse for them. They pushed God further and further away, choosing instead to worship the idols and false gods of the surrounding nations. The very people to whom the Israelites were supposed to shine the light of God snuffed out that flame and replaced it with a cheap, man-made imitation. God had singled them out to be His holy nation so that His name would be known throughout the earth and His salvation among all the nations (Psalm 67). He did many miraculous things and performed grand displays of His power so that His name would be revered (Psalm 22:7, Psalm 33:8). But their desire to be like everyone else got the best of them time and time again. Their time under the rule of an earthly king was no different than their time under the ruling of the judges. For over 400 years, they lived in the Promised Land under the rule of their kings. Some were good leaders, like David. David was Israel's second king and God called him "a man after God's own heart" (1 Samuel 13:14). David loved God and followed Him faithfully. He wrote many psalms, received revelations from God, and even made plans to build the first temple to God. God said to David:

The Lord Himself will establish a house for you; When your days are over and you rest with you ancestors, I will raise up your offspring to succeed you, who will come from your own body, and I will establish his kingdom. He is the one who will build a house for my Name, and I will establish the throne of his kingdom forever. I will be his father, and he will be my son...my love will never be taken away from him...Your house and your kingdom will endure forever before me; your throne will be established forever.

2 Samuel 7:11-16

God fulfilled this immediately through David's son Solomon, who is said to be the wisest man that ever lived. He wrote 3,000 proverbs and over 1,000 songs. Solomon completed the temple in Jerusalem, giving the presence of the Lord a permanent home. God used Solomon's wisdom and the temple to bring the nations in to see His glory through His chosen people. "From all nations people came to listen to Solomon's wisdom, sent by all the kings of the world, who had heard of his wisdom" (1 Kings 4:34).

Throughout Isaiah and also in the book of Romans, we read about the "Root of Jesse" or the "Branch of Jesse." Jesse was the father of king David and the root or branch of him is the fulfillment of the covenant God made with David in 2 Samuel 7:11-16.

But even David, the king after God's own heart, was imperfect and led a life plagued by sin and the consequences of it. Solomon as well, a man abundantly blessed with wisdom, wealth, and accomplishment beyond comprehension, was drawn away from God by the idol-worshipping masses around him. As the years went by and many kings came and went, God's people continued in their sinful rebellious ways and in doing so, moved further and further outside of His blessing and protection. Yet God always keeps His promises. Despite the fact that His people were not keeping up their end of the covenant, God never revoked His. The covenant He made with Abraham, Isaac, and Jacob, and then the covenant He made with David would both ultimately be fulfilled through one man. One King.

# DISCUSSION QUESTIONS

**1** David was a murderer and an adulterer. Yet history remembers him as "a man after God's own heart." If God can look past his sin and use David for His ultimate purposes, do you think He can do the same for you?

**2** Do you think God would call you a man or woman after His own heart? Why or why not?

**3** Have you seen any examples in your life or in the lives of family or friends where God has redeemed sinful choices and used them for His purposes? Discuss.

As for the foreigners who do not belong to your people Israel but have come from a distant land because of your name—for they will hear of your great name and your mighty hand and your outstretched arm—when they come and pray toward this temple, then hear from heaven, your dwelling place. Do whatever the foreigners ask of you, so that all the peoples of the earth may know your name and fear you, as do your own people Israel, and may know that this house I have built bears your Name. 1 Kings 8:41-43

~Solomon's prayer of dedication for the temple.

I have made you,

YOU ARE MY SERVANT;

ISRAEL,

I will not forget you.

Isaiah 44:21

# - SECTION 3 -
# SERVANTS OF
# THE LORD

The word 'servant' comes with many different connotations and it should because there are many different depictions of servants in this world. Throughout history and still today the word servant could apply to a human being unwillingly sold into slavery or an individual born into slavery through indentured service. It could also apply to well-paid and appreciated domestic help or an individual voluntarily serving through humility and love. The NIV Bible has the word 'servant' appearing 767 times, undoubtedly covering every picture and definition of servant that has ever existed. In Isaiah 49:3, God said, "You are my servant, Israel, in whom I will display my splendor." God's people were chosen to be a highly blessed and favored servant of the Lord. Another image of servant we see throughout the Old Testament is the prophet, the messengers of the Lord. The Old Testament wraps up with 17 books of prophecy, though there are somewhere between 50 and 80 people throughout the Bible that received prophesies, or messages from the Lord. Most of them had a very similar message: return to the Lord. Stop living for yourselves, stop worshipping idols and false gods, stop disregarding the laws of the Lord, and return to Him. Their messages were mostly met with the same reaction from God's people:

For these are rebellious people, deceitful children, children unwilling to listen to the Lord's instruction. They say to the seers, "See no more visions!" and to the prophets, "Give us no more visions of what is right!"

Isaiah 30:9-10

Eventually, the nation of Israel saw the fulfillment of God's threats in Joshua 23:14-15. Joshua had warned them from the very beginning:

> You know with all your heart and soul that none of all the good promises the Lord your God gave you has failed. Every promise has been fulfilled; not one has failed. But just as all the good things the Lord your God has promised you have come to you, so he will bring on you all the evil things he has threatened, until the Lord your God has destroyed you from this good land he has given you.

The fulfillment of this came in their exile from the Promised Land by the hands of the Assyrians and the Babylonians. God's servant, the nation of Israel, had failed. They "[had] not brought salvation to the earth, and the people of the world [had] not been reborn" (Isaiah 26:18). God's servants, the prophets, had failed at convincing the people to change their ways. He knew it would take a different kind of servant to bring His creation back to Him. Almost 700 years before Jesus, God told His people, through the prophet Isaiah, that He would send a servant who would not fail.

> Here is my servant, whom I uphold,
>     my chosen one in whom I delight;
> I will put my Spirit on him,
>     And he will bring justice to the nations.
> In faithfulness he will bring forth justice;
>     He will not falter or be discouraged
> till he establishes justice on earth.
>     In his teachings the islands will put their hope.

I will keep you and make you
    To be a covenant for the people
    And a light for the Gentiles,
To open eyes that are blind,
    To free captives from prison.
See, the former things have taken place,
    And new things I declare;
Before they spring into being
    I announce them to you.

Isaiah 42:1-2, 4, 6-7, 9

Jesus was foretold as more than a prophet, more than a servant. He was to be the Redeemer, the Messiah. God said "It is too small a thing for you to be my servant to restore the tribes of Jacob and bring back those of Israel I have kept. I will also make you a light for the Gentiles, that my salvation may reach to the ends of the earth" (Isaiah 49:6). Jesus was coming not simply to call the Israelites back to repentance. That was too small a task for the Son of God, the One who was with God since before the formation of earth. Jesus Himself was coming to do what nobody else could...He was coming to prove to the world once and for all that God loved them.

> Then the whole human race will know that I, the Lord, am your Savior, your Redeemer, the Mighty One of Jacob.
>
> Isaiah 49:26

93

# DISCUSSION QUESTIONS

**1** Read 2 Kings 17:7-23. Knowing the history of God's people, their rebellion, and the many warnings God sent through His prophets, does their punishment through exile seem justified?

**2** Do you think there's a difference between God punishing His people for their sin and Him simply allowing sin to bear its own consequences? Discuss the difference.

# LESSON 5
# FOR DEEPER STUDY

● Read the following verses in Psalms and reflect on the common theme:

– Psalm 9:11

– Psalm 18:49

– Psalm 22:22-23, 27-28

– Psalm 33:8

– Psalm 47:1-2

– Psalm 57:9-11

– Psalm 66:1-4

– Psalm 72:11, 17

● Read 1 Samuel 8:4-8, 19-20. Reflect on what God is saying about His people to the prophet Samuel.

- Ever since God rescued the Israelites from Egypt, His purpose was to set them apart (Exodus 19:5-6). How does the request of His people stand in direct opposition to this? (1 Samuel 8:19-20)

- Read Jeremiah 16:19-21. What is God saying the nations will do?

  – What will they be repentant of?

  – In verse 21, there is an action statement and a statement of purpose. What is the action and who is doing it? What is the purpose?

- Read Jeremiah 23:1-6. Who are the shepherds in this passage? Who is the flock?

  – Since the shepherds were not tending the flock with care, who did God say would gather the remnant of the flock? (v.3)

  – Who is the King and "righteous branch" He is foreshadowing in verses 5 and 6?

# SAVING GRACE

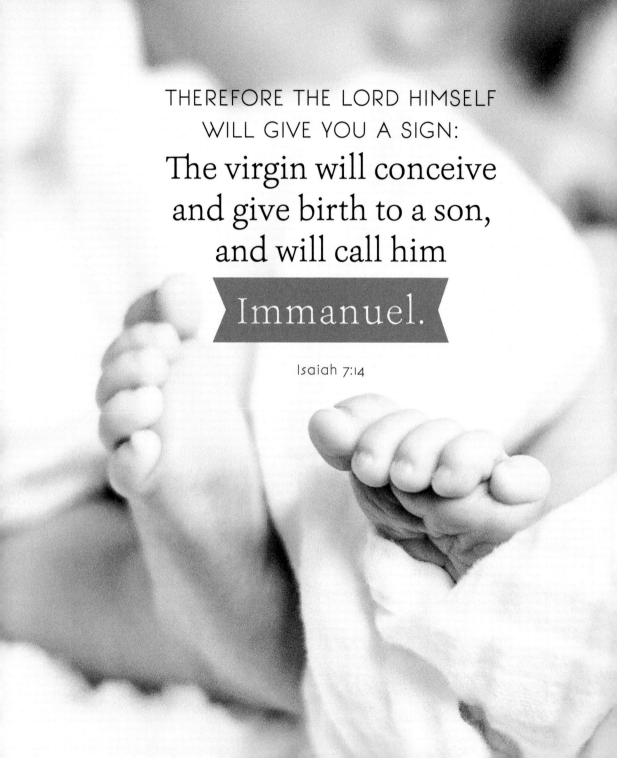

THEREFORE THE LORD HIMSELF
WILL GIVE YOU A SIGN:

The virgin will conceive
and give birth to a son,
and will call him

Immanuel.

Isaiah 7:14

# WHAT THE LAW COULD NOT DO

Relative to the history of the world, America is a very young country. Our roots here simply are not as deep as much of the rest of the world. If you were to trace your family line back as far as you could, you would not have to go very far before your search would take you to another country and nationality. Let's say your family is of Italian descent. Even if you were not born in Italy, you don't speak a single word of Italian (spaghetti does not count), you have never stepped foot on Italian soil, and you have absolutely no familial ties to Italy today, you could still call yourself Italian, or perhaps you would say you are of Italian descent. Your birth certificate, passport, and little to no knowledge of any language other than English all say that you are American, yet you are from the line of Italians and therefore, you can lay claim to that nationality. Furthermore, it was not because of any choice that you made that you are able to make that claim. You were simply born into it. In the same way, we are all descendants of Adam. Therefore, we were all born into the line of sin. Romans 5:19 says that "through the disobedience of the one man the many were made sinners." Yet in God's infinite grace and mercy, redemption was planned from the beginning. In our previous example, let's say that for whatever reason you decide to disassociate yourself with your Italian roots. You determine to not be Italian anymore. You could alter your appearance, change whatever cultural habits you've

> For just as through the disobedience of the one man the many were made sinners, so also through the obedience of the one man the many will be made righteous.
>
> Romans 5:19

grown up with, vow to never eat Italian again (what a pity that would be), and decide that you will definitely never set foot on Italian soil. Perhaps on the outside, you would succeed in convincing people of your changed nationality but there's really nothing you could do to actually rid yourself of your heritage. You would have to be born again into a different family line. Born again. If you've spent much time in church, you have probably heard that phrase before. It's sort of a Christian "buzz word" but what does it really mean? It means that in order to free His creation from the mess of sin we created and were born into, God needed to change our DNA. The law showed us what was good and holy but the law itself could not redeem His people because their DNA, our DNA, was still influenced by our sinful heritage. The law could only change what was on the outside, not what was on the inside. There was only one way and it required some drastic measures. God, the Creator of all things great and small, who sits on a throne in heaven amidst constant worship by the heavenly beings, humbled Himself, left His seat of honor and glory, and came down to be with us. He somehow managed to squeeze all of His glory into a tiny, sweaty, easily-tired, slowly decaying earth-suit. "For God was pleased to have all his fullness dwell in him, and through him to reconcile to himself all things" (Colossians 1:19-20). Isaiah foretold the day when Immanuel would come. Immanuel, meaning "God with us", was the only way. "The law of Moses was unable to save us because of the weakness of our sinful nature. So God did what the law could not do. He sent his own Son in a body like the bodies we sinners have. And in that body God declared an end to sin's control over us by giving his Son as a sacrifice for our sins" (Romans 8:3 NLT).

The people walking in darkness have seen a great light; on those living in the land of deep darkness a light has dawned...For to us a child is born, to us a son is given, and the government will be on his shoulders. And he will be called Wonderful Counselor, Mighty God, Everlasting Father,

Prince of Peace. Of the greatness of his government and peace there will be no end. He will reign on David's throne and over his kingdom, establishing and upholding it with justice and righteousness from that time on and forever. The zeal of the Lord Almighty will accomplish this.

Isaiah 9:2, 6-7

## DISCUSSION QUESTIONS

**1** What nationality were you born into? What significance, positive and negative, has that had on your life?

**2** How does it feel to know and understand that you were also born into the "heritage" of sin?

**3** Has your perception changed, positively or negatively, of the phrase "born-again Christian"? Would you label yourself as one? Why or why not?

In love a throne
will be established;
in faithfulness
a man will sit
on it – one from
the house of
David – one
who in judging
seeks justice
and speeds the
cause of
righteousness.

Isaiah 16:5

# - SECTION 2 -
# THE LIFE AND
# TEACHING OF JESUS

The Israelites had waited for centuries for the promised Messiah. The prophets of old had predicted that he would come and establish a new kingdom, one that would never end. But as is often the case in human understanding, their expectations of what a Messiah would look like were vastly different than the reality of God's plan. When Jesus came, the Israelites had long since returned to the Promised Land after many years of exile and rebuilt the temple under the faithful guidance of Nehemiah and Ezra. However, they were still not a free people, having been under the oppressive occupation of the Romans for quite some time. Jesus came neither as a powerful king that restored their freedom in the Promised Land nor as a victorious military leader who defeated the oppressing Roman army. He did not fit the bill of what they hoped for in a Messiah because they still misunderstood God's intentions for His chosen people. As we've seen from the beginning of this study, God wanted to use His people as a light to the nations. He desired to bless them so that they would bless others. Jesus reiterated this throughout his ministry. In Matthew chapters 5-7, Jesus gave his most famous sermon, the Sermon on the Mount. In it, he confirmed God's original plan for His chosen people while simultaneously turning everything in this world upside down. He said:

> You are the light of the world. A city on a hill cannot be hidden. Neither do people light a lamp and put it under a bowl. Instead they put it on its stand, and it gives light to everyone in the house. In the same way, let your light shine before others, that they may see your good deeds and glorify your Father in heaven.

Matthew 5:14-16

Jesus said "I must proclaim the good news of the kingdom of God... because that is why I was sent."

Luke 4:43

Some have described it as King Jesus' inaugural speech in which he explained what it is like to live as citizens in the kingdom of God. Jesus was on a mission to see the fulfillment of Revelation 7:9, a redeemed people from every nation, tribe, and tongue worshipping around the throne. He came to glorify His Father. He came to reconcile God's people to himself. Jesus came not to make better or improve God's people, but to make them an entirely new creation, free from the bonds of their sin nature, new from the inside out. He came so that God's people would see and know and touch and feel what it is like to live in the kingdom of God. His message was not "Here's how to enter the kingdom of God when you die." His message was "The Kingdom of God is here now!" (Luke 17:20-21) He taught that the kingdom of God could be here "on earth as it is in heaven" (Matthew 6:9-13). Jesus came to teach *and* to display the kingdom of God here on earth and that's exactly what he did. He traveled around the Promised Land performing miracles and great wonders and signs from God. He told people that the kingdom of God had come near (Mark 1:15, Matthew 4:23). Living for and in God's kingdom is not simply a matter of where you get to spend eternity. His focus was not "this is how you get to heaven when you die". In all that he did, his perfectly sinless life, his teachings, his sacrificial death, and his miraculous resurrection, Jesus ushered in the new kingdom of God here on earth. Kingdom living looks like loving the Lord your God "with all your heart, all your soul, and all your mind" and also "loving your neighbor as yourself" (Matthew 22:36-40). It looks like "faith expressing itself through love" (Galatians 5:6). It looks like "faith, hope, and love – and the greatest of these is love" (1 Corinthians 13:13). It looks like loving others as Christ loved us and in love "laying down one's life for others" (John 15:12-13). It looks like loving our enemies (Matthew 5:43-47). Do you see the theme here? As Isaiah said 700 years before Jesus, "In love a throne will be established." Jesus came to show God's people, ALL of God's people, that God is love. "For love comes

from God...anyone who does not love does not know God, *for God IS love*"
(1 John 4:7-8, emphasis added).

> "The Kingdom is God's total answer to man's total need."
> —E. Stanley Jones

# DISCUSSION QUESTIONS

 Read the parable of the tenants in Matthew 21:33-46. (It can also be found in Mark 12:1-12 and Luke 20:9-19.) As you read it, look for the following characters in the story: God, the Israelites, the prophets, the nations, and Jesus. Discuss the implications of the parable. (Hint: There's a cheat sheet below but see if you can identify them without looking first.)

## PARABLE OF THE TALENTS:

God is the landowner. Throughout scripture, you find the analogy of reaping and sowing, most often in regards to the lost and unreached (i.e. the nations) being portrayed as the harvest. The tenants in the story are the Israelites. Their job was to watch over the vineyard and "reap the harvest," or in other words bring the nations to the Lord. The servants in the story represent the prophets (Remember lesson 5, section 3?). When the prophets were sent, the Israelites rejected their messages and even killed many of them. ("The Israelites have rejected your covenant, torn down your altars, and put your prophets to death with the sword." 1 Kings 19:10) Finally at the end of the parable, the landowner sent his very own son. God sent His Son to do what the Israelites refused to do...bring home the harvest.

BUT HE WAS
PIERCED
for our transgressions,
HE WAS CRUSHED
FOR OUR INIQUITIES;
For the Lord has spoken:
the punishment
that brought us
PEACE
was on him,
AND BY HIS WOUNDS
we are healed.

Isaiah 53:5

## - SECTION 3 -
# DEATH AND RESURRECTION

With tears in her eyes, a little girl looks up from under the brim of her Easter hat and through sobs says, "But mommy, why did he have to die?" It's a heavy question. If you have ever seen a play or a movie accurately depict the passion and suffering of Christ, it is almost too much to bear. Of course, we have the benefit of knowing the end of the story...the Easter story. The tomb was empty, death was defeated, Jesus is risen! Yet it still leaves the question unanswered...why did Jesus have to die? If we rewind the story back a few hundred years, we see that it was always his purpose. Isaiah paints a very clear picture of the suffering servant, particularly in chapters 49-53. One of the clearest pictures of why Jesus had to die is shown in Isaiah 52:15. It says, "so he will sprinkle many nations, and kings will shut their mouths because of him. For what they were not told, they will see, and what they have not heard, they will understand." What does that mean, "he will sprinkle many nations"? Back in ancient Israel, when the priests would consecrate someone, or in other words make someone holy, they would sprinkle them with the blood of the sacrifice. You see, the Israelites knew from the beginning that whenever there was an offense committed against God, there needed to be a sacrifice. The sacrifice was a way of reconciling (or atoning) the sinner back to God. In Exodus and Leviticus, God outlined all the ways of sacrificially atoning for sin. Isaiah was saying that, many nations would be atoned for through Jesus. Kings would be left speechless that the King of Kings would sacrifice His

> After he has suffered, he will see the light of life and be satisfied; by his knowledge my righteous servant will justify many, and he will bear their iniquities.
>
> Isaiah 53:11

own Son for the sake of His people. And because of this, they would finally see and understand what they had previously not been told and had not heard. Through the suffering of Jesus, the nations would finally hear that God desires reconciliation with ALL of His people. Jesus came to serve, to suffer, and to die. The enemy knew this and in the very beginning of Jesus' ministry, he tried to convince Jesus that there was another way. In Matthew 4:1-11, Satan tried to tempt Jesus to take the easy way out, claiming that he did not have to serve (I will give you this kingdom if you simply worship me), he did not have to suffer (turn these stones to bread, you don't have to suffer hunger), and he did not have to die (throw yourself down, surely you will not die). But Jesus knew there was only one way, for He was with God in the beginning when they created the great redemption plan. That ominous Friday morning when Jesus walked through the streets of Jerusalem, suffering through the pain of a crown of thorns and the wounds of his flogging all across his back, when he carried his heavy cross through crowds that mocked him and spit at him, knowing what that cross meant, when he suffered what many historians say was the most excruciating and humiliating way to die...remember that he did this willingly, to redeem his people. "Greater love has no one than this: to lay down one's life for one's friends" (John 15:12).

How can we be sure that this was the only way, that this truly was the original plan of God? God revealed it hundreds of years earlier to His servant Isaiah, and hundreds of years prior to that to His servant David. As you read Psalm 22 in comparison to the actual description of Jesus' crucifixion found in the four gospels, consider this...David wrote this psalm hundreds of years before crucifixion was even invented.

| PSALM 22 | THE GOSPELS ACCOUNT OF THE DEATH OF JESUS |
|---|---|
| [16]Dogs surround me, a pack of villains encircles me; | "Then the governor's soldiers took Jesus into the Praetorium and gathered the whole company of soldiers around him." (Matthew 27:27) |
| [16b]they pierce my hands and my feet. | "Then they led him out to crucify him." (Matthew 27:35, Mark 15:20, Luke 22:33, John 19:18) |
| [17]All my bones are on display; people stare and gloat over me. | "The people stood watching, and the rulers even sneered at him." (Luke 23:35, Mark 15:29-32) |
| [18]They divide my clothes among them and cast lots for my garment. | "When they had crucified him, they divided up his clothes by casting lots." (Matthew 27:35, Mark 15:24, Luke 23:34, John 19:24) |
| [15]My mouth is dried up like a potsherd, And my tongue sticks to the roof of my mouth; | "Jesus said, "I am thirsty." A jar of wine vinegar was there, so they soaked a sponge in it, put the sponge on a stalk of the hyssop plant, and lifted it to Jesus' lips." (John 19:28) |
| [7]All who see me mock me; They hurl insults, shaking their heads. | "Those who passed by hurled insults at him, shaking their heads and saying, "You who are going to destroy the temple and build it in three days, save yourself!"" (Matthew 27:39, Mark 15:29) |
| [8]"He trusts in the Lord," [enemies] say, "let the Lord rescue him. Let him deliver him, since he delights in him." | The chief priests, teachers of the law, and elders said "He trusts in God. Let God rescue him now if he wants him, for he said, 'I am the Son of God.'" (Matthew 27:43) |

| PSALM 22 | THE GOSPELS ACCOUNT OF THE DEATH OF JESUS |
|---|---|
| ¹My God, my God, why have you forsaken me? | "About three in the afternoon Jesus cried out in a loud voice, "My God, my God, why have you forsaken me?"" (Matthew 27:46, Mark 15:34) |
| ³¹ᵇHe has done it! | "Jesus said, "It is finished." With that, he bowed his head and gave up his spirit." (John 19:30) |
| ¹⁴ I am poured out like water, and all my bones are out of joint. | "One of the soldiers pierced Jesus' side with a spear, bringing a sudden flow of blood and water." (John 19:34) |
| you lay me in the dust of death. | "Joseph took [Jesus'] body, wrapped it in a clean linen cloth, and placed it in his own new tomb that he had cut out of a rock." (Matthew 27:60, Mark 15:46, Luke 23:53-54, John 19:39-42) |
| ²⁷All the ends of the earth will remember and turn to the Lord, and all the families of the nations will bow down before him, ²⁸for dominion belongs to the Lord and he rules over the nations. ³¹They will proclaim his righteousness, declaring to a people yet unborn: | "Then Jesus came to them and said, "All authority in heaven and on earth has been given to me. Therefore go and make disciples of all nations, baptizing them in the name of the Father and the Son and the Holy Spirit, and teaching them to obey everything I have commanded you. And surely I am with you always, to the very end of the age."" (Matthew 28:18-19) |

# LESSON 6
# FOR DEEPER STUDY

- Read Romans 11:11-32. Paul is making the argument that salvation has come to the Gentiles in order to make Israel envious. What does he say is the purpose of that? (v. 14)

  - Is Paul saying that Israel has been forever separated from God, that God has revoked their calling as a light to the nations? (v. 29)

  - When does he say that the Israelites will return to the Lord and be saved? (v. 25)

  - What do you think he means in verse 32?

- Read Luke 4:14-27. When Jesus stood up to read, as was his custom, he found a verse in Isaiah. In your own words, what was the message of what he read? (v. 18-19)

  - What did he say was the significance of that scripture? (v. 21)

  - What was the reaction at that point from the people in the synagogue?

  - Jesus then refers to the story of the prophet Elijah coming to the aid of a non-Israelite widow, a story found in 1 Kings 17:8-24. What is the outcome of that story? (1 Kings 17:24)

  - What was he pointing out to the people in the synagogue in verse 26?

- He then refers to the story of the prophet Elisha going out of his way to heal Naaman, a Syrian and therefore not an Israelite. (2 Kings 5:1-17) What was the outcome of that story? (2 Kings 5:15)

- This all took place in Nazareth, Jesus' hometown. What was it about what Jesus said to the people in the synagogue that made them go from admiration in verse 22 to extreme anger in verses 28-29?

● What does Jesus say is the reason he was sent?

    – Luke 4:43

    – Mark 13:9-11 (NLT)

    – John 12:32

    – John 17:18

● Read Matthew 10:5-7. Jesus sent out the 12 disciples to the Jews first. Why do you think that was his strategy?

    – The original 12 (the 12 tribes of Israel) were "blessed to be a blessing". With that in mind, what do you think Jesus was trying to accomplish through his chosen 12?

● Read and reflect on these stories of Jesus' interaction with non-Jewish people. What was the outcome of them all?

– Jesus and the Gerasene demoniac (Mark 5:1-20)

– Jesus and the Roman Centurion (Matthew 8:5-13)

– Jesus and the Canaanite Woman (Matthew 15:21-28)

– Jesus and the Samaritan Woman (John 4:1-26, 39-42)

LESSON 7

# THE STORY CONTINUES

Give praise to the Lord,
CALL ON HIS NAME; MAKE KNOWN AMONG
THE NATIONS WHAT HE HAS DONE,
and proclaim that his name is exalted.
Sing to the Lord,
for he has done
glorious things;
LET THIS BE KNOWN TO
ALL THE WORLD.

ISAIAH 12:4-5

# - SECTION 1 -
# THE GREAT
# COMMISSION

In the book "The Forgotten God" by Francis Chan, he poses the question "If you could choose between Jesus beside you and the Holy Spirit within you, which would you choose?" If you would say Jesus beside you, Francis would say that you probably do not truly understand the power of the Holy Spirit.* Don't beat yourself up though, the original disciples of Jesus did not understand either. Jesus predicted his death and resurrection multiple times to his disciples but they did not understand. In one such prediction, he even tells them why it would happen: "And I, when I am lifted up from the earth, will draw all people to myself" (John 12:32). In the chapters that follow, Jesus continues to explain to his followers what must happen and they continue to *not* understand him. But Jesus said to them "very truly I tell you, it is for your good that I am going away. Unless I go away, the Advocate will not come to you; but if I go, I will send him to you" (John 16:7). The Advocate is the Holy Spirit, the third member of the trinity, the equal yet often "forgotten" God. This is how God was going to change His people. Through Jesus, He made a way for His very Spirit to dwell in the hearts of His followers. Jesus Himself said that it was *better* for Him to go away so that instead we could have the Holy Spirit! After the resurrection, John records two things of significance in the first meeting with the resurrected Jesus. In John 20:21-22, Jesus appears to His disciples for the first time after the resurrection and says ""Peace be with you! As the Father has sent me, I am sending you." And with that he breathed on them and said, 'Receive the Holy Spirit.'" Jesus gave them His Spirit and He sent them out as the Father had sent Him. Just before the crucifixion, Jesus alluded (again) to the way and purpose with which He had been sent by the Father. In John 17:4, in praying to the Father, Jesus said "I have brought you

*Francis Chan and Danae Yankoski, *Forgotten God: Reversing Our Tragic Neglect of the Holy Spirit* (David C. Cook, 2009)

On this mountain
he will destroy the
shroud that enfolds all
peoples, the sheet that
covers all nations; he will
swallow up death forever.
The Sovereign Lord will
wipe away the tears from
all faces; he will
remove his people's
disgrace from all
the earth.

Joshua 24:13-15

glory on earth by finishing the work you gave me to do." That work was to point people back to a loving Father, to make a way for redemption and reconciliation with Him. He ushered in a new kingdom, a kingdom characterized by life, love, and hope, not death and despair. The resurrection of Jesus was the first-fruit of this new Kingdom. It loudly proclaimed for the ages that death had been defeated! When Adam and Eve first disobeyed God and brought sin and death into the world, God vowed to redeem His people and make right what they had made wrong. Now we as believers have the opportunity to co-labor with Jesus to fulfill God's ultimate purpose, which is to see redeemed people from every nation, tribe, and tongue worshipping around the throne. When Jesus first told his disciples that he was leaving, they asked when he would return. He stated very clearly "this gospel of the kingdom will be preached in the whole world as a testimony to all nations, *and then the end will come*" (Matthew 24:14, emphasis added). As we have looked at from the beginning, God has one goal... to redeem people from every nation. In case it was not clear, Jesus put the final emphasis on this calling in His very last statement here on earth. Just before He ascended up to heaven where He took His seat at the right hand of God, He gave one final and all-encompassing command to His followers: "Go and make disciples of all nations, baptizing them in the name of the Father, and of the Son, and of the Holy Spirit, and teaching them to obey everything I have commanded you. And surely I am with you always, to the very end of the age" (Matthew 28:19). This is the Great Commission, also known as the Great Co-Mission. God has called every single one of us to participate in the most important task in God's Kingdom...redeeming His people to Himself.

# DISCUSSION QUESTIONS

**1** What do you think of when you read the word "missions"?

**2** Do you think that all believers have a role to play in missions? Why or why not?

**3** Some might say that Matthew 28:19 is just for the people that are called to overseas missions. Others would argue that as Jesus' last words to His disciples, they were meant for all of His followers. What do you believe and has that changed since the beginning of this study?

"And the gospel must first be preached to all nations."
~Jesus (Mark 13:10)

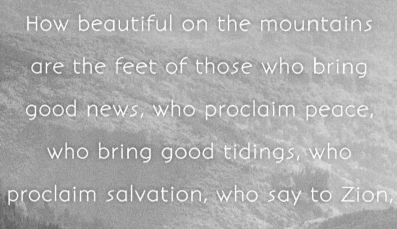

How beautiful on the mountains
are the feet of those who bring
good news, who proclaim peace,
who bring good tidings, who
proclaim salvation, who say to Zion,

"Your God reigns!"

Isaiah 52:7

# - SECTION 2 -
# THE WORK OF THE APOSTLES

After Jesus' death and resurrection, His disciples still could not quite grasp the concept of God's Kingdom here on earth. The book of Acts (which is the first book after the four gospels and named as such for the 'acts of the apostles') opens up with Jesus' ascension into heaven. He said to his followers, "Do not leave Jerusalem, but wait for the gift my Father promised, which you have heard me speak about. For John baptized with water, but in a few days you will be baptized in the Holy Spirit" (Acts 1:4-5). It is probably safe to assume that they had no idea what that meant. They proceeded to ask Jesus "Lord, are you at this time going to restore the kingdom to Israel?" (v.6) They still, after all this time, all the miracles, all the parables, the death, and the resurrection thought that Jesus' purpose was to restore what once was. But Jesus did not come to restore the old, He came to make something new.  Just as Isaiah predicted, "Forget the former things; do not dwell on the past. See, I am doing a new thing!" (Isaiah 43:18-19). The new thing began with God's own Spirit coming to dwell in the hearts of every believer, going out and proclaiming the good news to the ends of the earth (Acts 1:8), and coming to completion in the form of "members of every tribe and language and people and nation" being redeemed to the Lord their God (Revelation 5:9).  The apostles couldn't help but share what they had witnessed and experienced in walking with Jesus. On the day of Pentecost alone, after they received the Holy Spirit and began speaking in many different tongues, there were 3,000

Then I heard the voice of the Lord saying, "Whom shall I send? And who will go for us?" And I said, "Here am I. Send me!"

Isaiah 6:8

new believers that very day (Acts 2:41). The message of the gospel was so compelling that Luke, the writer of Acts, goes on to say that "the Lord added to their number daily those who were being saved" (Acts 2:47). They were arrested and persecuted by the same people who crucified Jesus. They were told to stop speaking about Jesus or suffer the same fate. On one such occasion, Peter and John were commanded to stop teaching about Jesus and they replied to their persecutors, "we cannot help speaking about what we have seen and heard" (Acts 4:20). This is how compelling the gospel of Jesus Christ is! Stephen, one of the early believers, was stoned to death for it. Saul, who later became Paul, was completely changed by it. Upon hearing the gospel, he went from the most fervent persecutor of Christians to eventually the author of most of the New Testament. They were arrested, flogged, beaten, killed by the sword, some killed in the same manner of Jesus, and yet they did not let up in sharing their faith. The writer of Hebrews says "the world was not worthy of them" (Hebrews 11:38). Because of their adamant testimony to the life, death, and resurrection of Jesus, the gospel spread like wildfire. Within the lifetime of these eyewitnesses, the good news had traveled throughout parts of Europe, Asia, and Africa. Paul traveled all over that region of the world, sailing all the way from Jerusalem to Rome, enduring shipwreck, trials, and multiple prison sentences. In fact, many of the books of the New Testament were actually letters written from an imprisoned Paul to churches that he had started in other cities. It is because of the faith of these men and women, and their commitment to God's purpose of redeeming His people back to Himself, the we can sit halfway across the globe over 2,000 years after the fact and study the teachings of Jesus.

# ACTIVITY

Compare Isaiah 61:8-9 below, sometimes referred to as the Messianic Covenant, with the Abrahamic Covenant (Genesis 12:2-3) we looked at back in Lesson 2, Section 2. What are the similarities? What are the differences?

In my faithfulness I will reward my people

and make an everlasting covenant with them.

Their descendants will be known among the nations

and their offspring among the peoples.

All who see them will acknowledge

that they are a people the Lord has blessed.

Isaiah 61:8-9

# DISCUSSION QUESTIONS

**1** In Acts 2:41, it says that 3,000 new believers were added to them in a single day. Do you think the gospel of Jesus is that compelling today? Why or why not? Do you think the gospel has changed or are we perhaps missing something in our understanding of it?

**2** What do you think it would be like to experience the emotions of Peter and John in Acts 4:20 when they said that they couldn't help speaking about what they had seen and heard? Do you now or have you ever felt that way about the gospel? Have you ever known someone that has? Describe what a life characterized by those emotions looks like.

And I, because of what they have planned and done, am about to come and gather the people of all nations and languages, and **they will come and see my glory.**

Isaiah 66:18

# - SECTION 3 -
# WHERE ARE
# WE TODAY?

It was June 6, 1944. The Allied forces launched the largest seaborne invasion in history. Within a week, the beaches of Normandy were under Allied control and the door to victory had been opened. This intricately planned operation began the liberation of German-occupied northwestern Europe during World War II and was the turning point of the war. Many people consider this day, now called D-day, the day the Allies won the war. However, the fighting continued as the troops marched across Europe, gaining more ground with every city, country, and military base. Then on May 7, 1945 Germany surrendered and with that surrender came the official end of World War II in Europe. We now commemorate the victory by celebrating V-E day, or Victory in Europe day, May 8. Even though the war was essentially won on D-day, there were still many battles to be fought between then and V-E day.

As followers of Jesus, we have already had our D-day. It didn't happen on the beaches of Normandy, it happened on a cross on Calvary.* When Jesus humbled himself to death on a cross, bearing the punishment we deserved, and then defeating death by his resurrection from the dead, He won the war. The war against a very strong enemy, an evil opposition that wants the allegiance of God's people for himself. Although victory is assured, we have not yet reached our V-E day. There are still many battles to be fought, many territories that have yet to be freed from the oppression of the enemy. The amazing thing

> The Spirit of the Sovereign Lord is on me, because the Lord has anointed me to proclaim good news.
>
> Isaiah 61:1

*Analogy borrowed from Ken Blue, *Authority to Heal* (1979)

is God has enlisted us to co-mission with Him in freeing the oppressed and sharing the Good News of freedom and life abundant! Jesus commissioned us to preach this gospel of His to the ends of the earth. He said he would not come back until this had been accomplished (Matthew 24:14). He assured us the V-E day would come but not until every captive had an opportunity to experience freedom here on earth.

In the Great Commission (Matthew 28:19), our English Bibles translate the word "ethne" into nations. It can be a little misleading because we might think geo-political nations, like the United States. However, the word "ethne" is more accurately translated to "people groups." We define people groups as groups of people that share the same culture, language, beliefs, and ethnicity. As an example, the United States in not one ethne, it is actually composed of over 480 unique people groups. This definition of people groups is consistent with the original meaning of "all peoples on earth" in the original promise to Abraham in Genesis 12:2-3, as well as the fulfillment of the promise in Revelation 7:9. Amazingly, with modern technology, we now have the ability to define, count, and track "people groups" throughout the planet.

So if V-E day is contingent on every one of them hearing the Good News, how are we doing?

- According to TheTravelingTeam.org, there are currently 16,761 uniquely identified people groups in the world. Of those, 7,050 are defined as unreached, meaning their population consists of less than 2% evangelical Christians.

- Looking at those statistics, 42% of the world has likely never heard the gospel of Jesus. We have barely crossed the halfway mark of The Great Commission.

- Of the roughly 3 billion people that fall within the definition of "unreached," 2.75 billion of them live within the geographical window known as the 10/40 window. This window stretches across north Africa, the middle east, and southeast Asia between the latitudinal lines of 10° and 40° above the equator.

- According to Wycliff.org, there are approximately 7,000 languages in use around the world today. Of those, there are still around 1,800 languages that do not have a Bible in their own language.

- Only about 6.4% of money given to Christian causes goes to global missions. That equates to about $45 billion, which is about the same amount Americans spend every year on dieting programs.

- Less than 1% of all money given to Christian causes goes towards reaching the unreached. That equates to about the same as what Americans typically spend on Halloween costumes...for their pets.

- Less than 4% of Christian missionaries worldwide are working with unreached people groups. That is 1 Christian missionary for every 216,300 unreached people.

- There are 78,000 evangelical Christians in the world for every single unreached people group.

- The American church has roughly 3,000 times the financial resources and 9,000 times the manpower needed to finish the Great Commission.

"This operation is not being planned with any alternatives. This operation is planned as a victory, and that's the way it's going to be. We're going down there, and we're throwing everything we have into it, and we're going to make it a success."

~General Dwight D. Eisenhower of the Normandy Landings

In Luke 10:2, Jesus said to his disciples, "The harvest is plentiful but the workers are few. Ask the Lord of the harvest, therefore, to send out workers into his harvest field." Sharing the good news of the gospel is not about who is right and who is wrong. It is not about forcing one's opinion and beliefs on others. It's simply the way we shine a light onto our Heavenly Father. In the same way that the Israelites were set apart to bring the nations back into a redeemed relationship with the Creator, we as followers of Jesus are now the torchbearers. We have been set apart to shine the light of Jesus, the means for redemption with the Father, into the nations. We have been made holy and blameless through the sacrificial love of Jesus so that we could become the dwelling place of God. Through His indwelling Spirit, we have the incredible honor and privilege of co-missioning with the Father in order to see His greatest purpose fulfilled...bringing His children home.

# FOR DEEPER STUDY

● As you have probably seen by now, God's heart for the nations is a story woven throughout the entire Bible. My prayer is that you would dive back into the Scriptures, from Genesis to Revelation, and see for yourself how God has written His story throughout every book of the Bible.

For more information on God's heart for the nations and His global purpose, look into the following:

- Perspectives on the Worldwide Christian Movement. Experience God's heart for all peoples and encounter the momentum of the World Christian Movement at www.perspectives.org.

- *God's Heart for the Nations* by Jeff Lewis, an inductive Bible study on God's heart for the world

- Visit nicoleparkswrites.com for more resources and information on God's heart for the nations.

# NEXT STEPS

As we have seen, missions began in the heart of God, not in the heart of man. It is not something that we decide for ourselves *if* we will participate. Rather, it is something that every follower of Jesus seeks to understand *how* he or she is called to participate. Jesus' last words to his followers were "Go and make disciples of all nations" (Matthew 28:19). There is more than one way to 'go and make disciples'. God has specifically gifted and blessed each person in accordance with his or her role in the Great Commission. How has God blessed you? How has He gifted you? How can those gifts and blessings be used for His ultimate goal of redeeming all nations to himself? Look through this list of ways that Christians can be involved in God's global mission and pray that He would reveal how He has called you to participate.

1 – PRAY FOR THE NATIONS   Every follower of Jesus should join in asking the God of the harvest to send more workers. (Matthew 9:37-38, Luke 10:2) We can all intercede on behalf of those who have not yet heard the Good News. For more information on the unreached people groups around the world, visit JoshuaProject.net or TheTravelingTeam.org. You can also sign up to receive daily devotional emails with different unreached people groups (UPGs) at www.GlobalPrayerDigest.org.

2 – GO TO THE NATIONS   There are innumerable opportunities to go to the nations and put names and faces to the statistics. Start with a short-term trip through your church. Pray about whether or not God might be asking you to serve abroad in some capacity. If you've been on a short-term trip and feel ready to take the next step, visit www.Cafe1040.com for more information on an overseas mentorship or getting connected with a sending agency for more long-term work.

3 – SEND TO THE NATIONS  Not everybody can go and not everybody wants to go. By financially supporting those who go, you can be an active and essential part of God's global plan. Find a missionary that shares your heart for a certain location or people group and join their support team. Ask your church how you can financially support short- and long-term missions at your home church. You can also partner financially with organizations that work solely on bringing the Gospel to the unreached, like Cafe 1040. (www.cafe1040.com/give)

4 – WELCOME INTERNATIONALS  You do not have to go overseas to find the nations. God brings the nations to us through international students, workers, refugees, and immigrants. It is estimated that there are over 886,000 international students in the U.S. and 80% of them will return home without ever having been invited into an American home. Whether you live in a big city, small town, or college town, look for opportunities to welcome internationals and be the hands and feet of Jesus right in your own backyard.

5 – MOBILIZE TO THE NATIONS  In the English language, the word 'mobilize' is primarily used in the context of the military. It refers to the logistics of moving assets, supplies, soldiers, and weapons to wherever the need is greatest. Mobilizing in the context of missions is helping people see the need for missions, understand God's heart for the nations, and get the resources and the people to the place of greatest need: the unreached. You can do this by sharing with others what you learned in this study, encouraging others to do this study, and helping people see the importance of global missions. For more ideas and resources on mobilization, visit www.mobilization.org.

# LEADER GUIDE

This study is divided into 7 lessons and each lesson has 3 sub-sections. Each of the sections has a small reading that frames and gives context to the topic of the lesson. Each section is then followed by discussion questions. Having participants do the reading and think about the discussion questions before coming to the meeting will facilitate better conversation.

At the end of every lesson, there is a section for deeper study. Depending on your group, you may want to include this in the discussion. These questions and reading assignments are meant to facilitate a deeper dive into the Scriptures. It can be an optional part of the study but the experience will be much richer with the deeper study, regardless of whether or not it is included in the discussion.

The study is written as a 7-week (or 7 meeting) group study. Before every meeting, participants would typically do the reading, questions, and deeper study for the entire lesson. The sub-sections within the lessons are meant to help guide conversation through the topics while going chronologically through the Bible without being overwhelming.

If you are doing this study outside of a group setting, it can be done the same way or as a 21-day devotional study. In that case, you would do one sub-section per day.

Regardless of how it is facilitated, here are some overarching questions to consider in each lesson.

- What do the stories in this lesson tell you about mankind? What do they tell you about God?

- How do the verses highlighted from Isaiah highlight/reiterate God's purposes and/ or foreshadow Jesus?

- What do you like about this lesson? What, if anything, feels challenging?

- How has this affected your perception and understanding of the Bible, God, Jesus, and the Gospel?

- What will you do with this information? Who will you share it with?

# NOTES

# NOTES